LET'S INVESTIGATE
Circles

LET'S INVESTIGATE
Circles

By Marion Smoothey

Illustrated by Ted Evans

MARSHALL CAVENDISH
NEW YORK · LONDON · TORONTO · SYDNEY

Library Edition Published 1993

© Marshall Cavendish Corporation 1993

Published by Marshall Cavendish Corporation
2415 Jerusalem Avenue
PO Box 587
North Bellmore
New York 11710

Series created by Graham Beehag Book Design

Library of Congress Cataloging-in-Publication Data

Smoothey, Marion, 1943-
  Circles/ by Marion Smoothey; illustrated by Ted Evans.
    p. cm.. -- (Let's Investigate)
  Includes index.
  Summary: Introduces the importance and uses of circles through a variety of problems, games, and activities.
  ISBN 1-85435-456-6 ISBN 1-85435-455-8 (set)
  1. Circle -- Juvenile literature. [1. Circle. 2. Geometry. 3. Mathematical recreations.] I. Evans, Ted ill. II. Title. III. Series:
  Smoothey, Marion, 1943- Let's Investigate.
  QA484.566 1992   92-7159
  516.22---dc20   CIP
                                                       AC

Printed in Singapore by Times Offset PTE Ltd
Bound in the United States

Contents

Circle shapes were probably among the first things you saw when you opened your eyes this morning. You may have looked at a clock to check the time, turned a knob to hear the radio or you may have drawn the curtains and seen the sun, if you were lucky.

● Make a list of the circles you can see around you now. Objects such as balls are spheres because they are three-dimensional. Mathematical circles have no thickness, but for the moment count things which have a circular edge like the rim of a can or a button.

Some circles, such as the edge of the yellow center of a daisy or the pupil of your eye, will be natural. Others, like plates and dials, will be made by people. Divide your list into these two sorts of circle to find out which kind you saw most of.

● Now try to draw a circle with just a pencil and paper. It's difficult, isn't it? Yet people use the circle shape for so many of the things they make.

● Can you think of some of the advantages and disadvantages of circles? Start a list now and add to it as you discover more from reading this book and trying out the activities in it.

Parts of the Circle

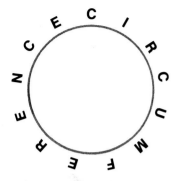

In order to talk accurately about circles, you need to learn the names for their parts.

7

Circumference

The **circumference** is the distance around the edge of a circle. "*Circum*" is a Latin word meaning "around;" if you circumnavigate the world, you sail all the way around it.

In the sixteenth century, a Portuguese seafarer, Ferdinand Magellan, led the first expedition to circumnavigate the globe. He died before the end of his journey but his ships sailed west from Spain, around South America, where the Strait of Magellan bears his name, across the Pacific and back to Spain.

Arcs

An arc is part of the circumference. If the circumference is cut into two unequal arcs, the larger is called the major arc and the smaller the minor arc.

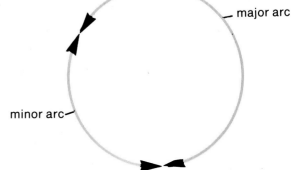

major arc

minor arc

Radii and Sectors

A **radius** is the distance from the center of the circle to any point on the circumference.

The spokes of a bicycle wheel **radiate** from the hub to the rim.

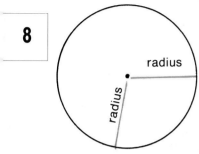

A circle has an infinite number of radii all of the same length. You can imagine drawing them in with a magically fine pencil and leaving tiny spaces between them.

The part of a circle between two radii is a **sector**. Each two radii will cut the circle into a major sector and a minor sector.

Diameter

A **diameter** of a circle is any line passing through the center from one point on the circumference to another point on the circumference.

A diameter cuts a circle into two semicircles. The length of the diameter of a particular circle is twice the length of the radius of that circle.

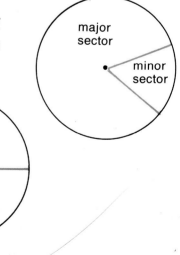

A searchlight radiates a beam of light.

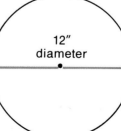

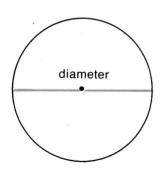

1

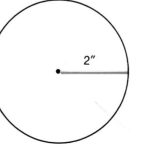

2

12″
diameter

1. What is the length of the diameter of this circle?

2. How long is the radius?

Chord and Segments

A straight line joining two points on the circumference of a circle is a **chord**.

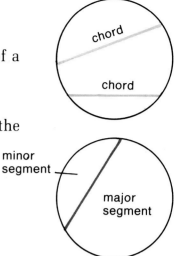

● Is the diameter a chord?

A chord cuts a circle into two **segments** which are called the major and minor segments.

You can remember that a segment looks like a segment of an orange standing on its straight side.

Draw around a plate on a piece of paper and cut out the circle. Fold the circle in half so that the edges fit on top of each other exactly. Open the circle. The fold line you have made is a diameter of the circle.

● How can you use folding to find the center of the circle?
● What is the least number of folds you need to make?

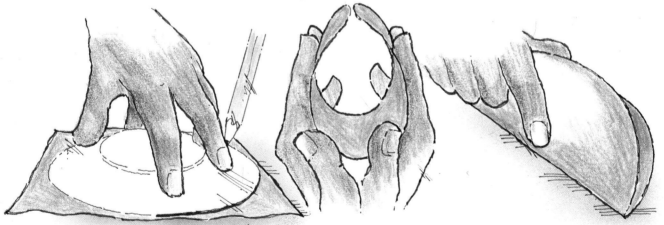

Cut out another circle. Make two marks on the circumference. Fold the circle so that the marks are on top of each other. What is the name of the fold line?

● Does this work wherever you place the marks on the circumference?

Ways of Drawing a Circle

Puzzle one

If you were asked to draw a circle on a piece of paper without a compass, your first idea would probably be to draw around a circular object such as a coin or a lid. Suppose you were asked to use only a thumbtack, a strip of cardboard and a sharpened pencil. How would you do it?

When you have thought out your answer or experimented, turn to page 12.

Puzzle two

You have landed on an unexplored planet and are trying to explain to the inhabitants where you have come from. If you had two pointed sticks and a piece of string, how could you draw circles in the dusty surface of the planet to represent the solar system?

Look at page 15 if you think you know how to do it.

Drawing a circle with a ruler and pencil

1. On a piece of paper, mark a cross where you would like the center of your circle. Place your ruler against the cross and draw a line about 2″ long along the other edge of the ruler.

2. Turn the ruler slightly and draw the next line.

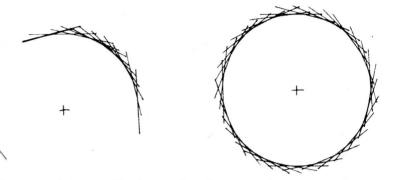

3. Repeat this until the ruler has made a complete turn around the point.

4. It is important to make lots of small turns. Try making big ones and see what happens.

● How would you make a smaller or larger circle?

● What is the connection between the radius of the circle you drew and the ruler you used?

● Suppose you only had a piece of paper. Could you make a circle by tearing and folding? The diagrams should give you a clue.

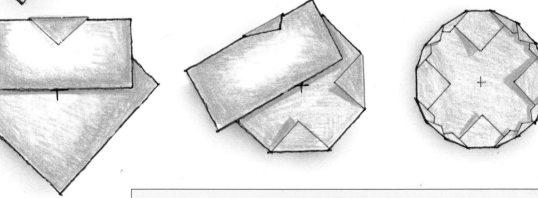

Turn to page 13.

Drawing a circle with thumbtack, cardboard and pencil.

1. Push the thumbtack through one end of the strip of cardboard to make a hole large enough for the point of the pencil.

12

2. Fasten the other end of the strip of cardboard to the paper with the thumbtack.

3. Holding the tack in position with one hand, push the pencil around in a circle.

4. The length of the cardboard between the two holes becomes the radius of the circle.

If you figured this out, turn back to page 11.
If it had you stumped, try the other puzzle on page 10.

Drawing circles the easy way

The circle is the basis of many attractive patterns. If you want to copy some of the patterns in this book or to create your own, you need the proper tool for the job – a compass.

If you are not familiar with using a compass, take some time to practice on scrap paper before trying a complicated pattern. The patterns on page 14 are good ones with which to start.

Handy hints

● **Use a ruler and your compass to mark off and set to the required radius. (Remember that the radius is half of the diameter of the finished circle.)**

● **Make sure that the screw holding the arms of the compass is tight enough to hold them firmly in position as you draw around the circumference of your circle.**

● **Adjust the pencil so that it touches the paper with the compass held nearly upright.**

● **Holding the top of the compass between your thumb and forefinger, gently rotate it.**

● **Don't try to turn the pencil by holding it.**

● **Don't worry if you don't get all the way around in one sweep. As long as the arms of your compass are kept at the same distance apart and you put the point back in the same place, you can stop and start again.**

● **Use a sharp pencil and don't go over the lines in felt pens: this defeats the purpose of using the compass.**

● You can achieve the effect of interlocking rings, like the Olympic symbol.

1. Draw overlapping pairs of circles.

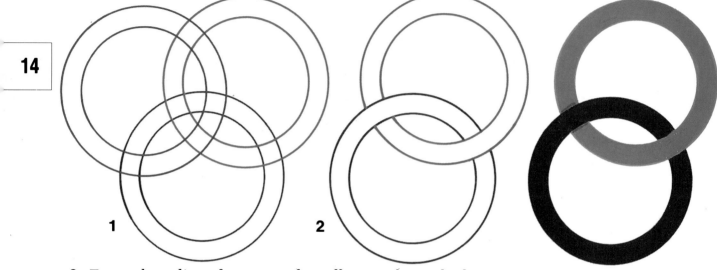

1   **2**

2. Erase these lines for an overlap effect so that it looks as though one circle first goes over and then under the other.

● It is a good idea to practice with just two rings. Then you can have fun making intricate designs with many circles.

● The "beach ball" effect is achieved by combining two patterns based on semicircles. Study the diagrams and see if you can copy it.

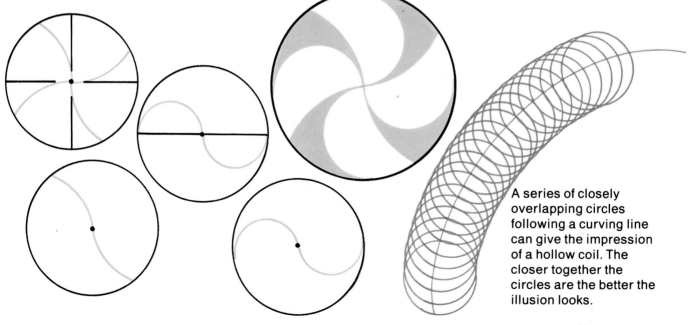

A series of closely overlapping circles following a curving line can give the impression of a hollow coil. The closer together the circles are the better the illusion looks.

14

Drawing a circle with sticks and string

1. Tie each end of the string around a stick.

2. Set one stick firmly in the ground.

3. Holding the string taut, move the other stick around in a circle.

It is important to keep the string tight because this is the radius of the circle. You can adjust the length of the string to draw different sized circles.

Turn back to page 11.

Circle Patterns

A useful fact

16

If you draw a circle and then, keeping the same radius, mark off around the circumference, you will find that the radius fits in around the circumference 6 times. This works whatever the size of the circle and can be used as the basis for many pretty patterns.

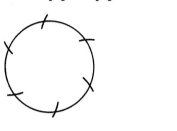

● There are some examples below for you to copy, but it is much more fun to make up your own. If a group of you get together, you can make a very nice wall display. Or you might choose one to be your personal logo to decorate your books.

More complicated circle patterns

Erasing some of the lines creates attractive effects.

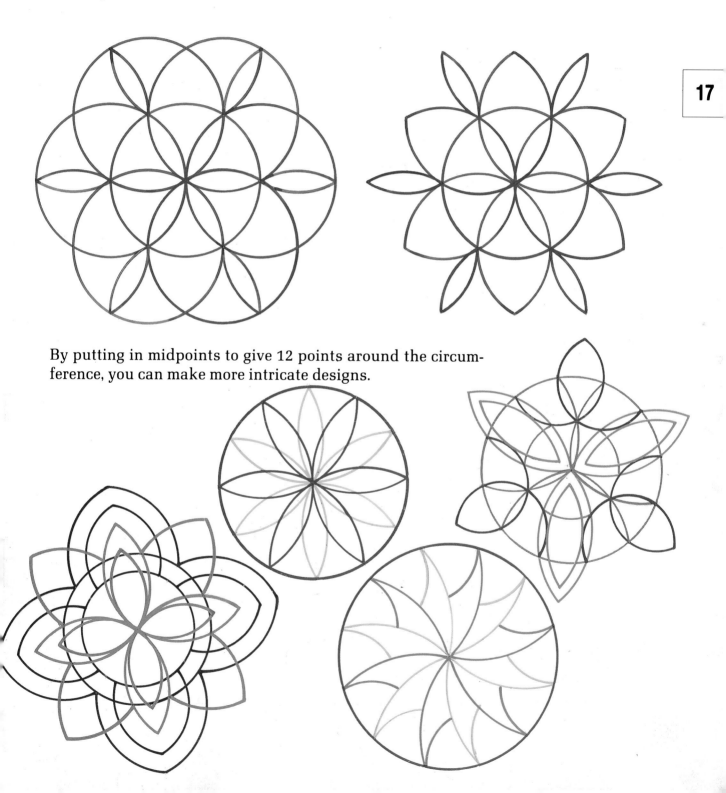

By putting in midpoints to give 12 points around the circumference, you can make more intricate designs.

You can use just one color and leave white space to make a good looking and complicated design.

This design uses circles passing through 12 points on the circumference of the base circle. A radius of 2″ gives a finished pattern with a radius of 8″ which is easy to color in.

Concentric circles

Circles of different radii which share the same center are **concentric**. When you throw a pebble into a still pond, the ripples it makes are concentric circles.

● You can make some interesting three-dimensional and spiral effects by combining concentric circles, straight lines and shading.

These patterns work best if the concentric circles increase in radius at regular intervals. Making the radius $\frac{1}{4}''$ larger each time is about right. Marking off around the circumference with a protractor at 10 degree intervals can be the basis for spiral effects or you can use regularly spaced horizontal or vertical lines.

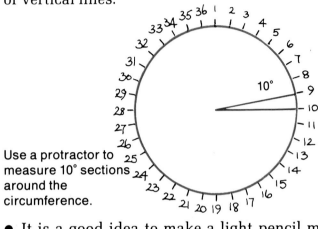

Use a protractor to measure 10° sections around the circumference.

● It is a good idea to make a light pencil mark in each section you are going to shade. These patterns are quite time-consuming to draw and mistakes can be very disappointing.

● Try not to mark your circles and lines too heavily or they will distract the eye from your finished design.

These patterns, called Catherine wheels, are based on concentric circles.

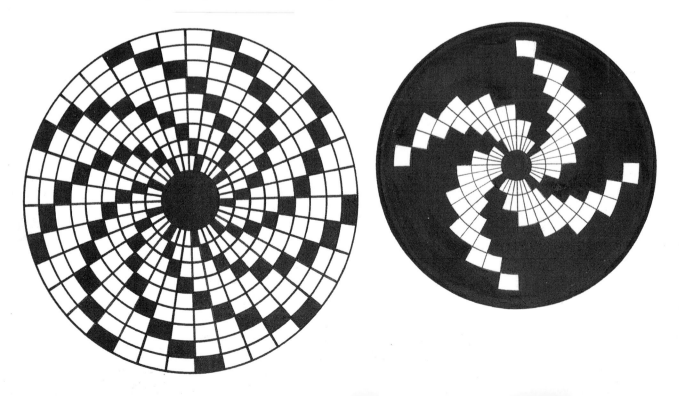

Using Circles to Make Other Shapes

21

An ellipse from a circle

Method 1

You need a pencil, compass, ruler and set square. If you do not have a set square, you can make one from folding a thin piece of cardboard twice, as shown in the illustrations left.

1. Draw a circle. Mark a point P inside it but not at the center. Lightly draw any chord which passes through P. Use your set square to draw in heavily the **perpendiculars** from the points where the chord meets the circumference.

2. Lightly draw another chord passing through P and mark clearly the perpendiculars where it meets the circumference. Repeat this many times until the ellipse appears.

Method 2

Draw a circle with a radius of 4″. Mark a point P inside it but not at the center. Cut out the circle. Make a series of folds so that a different point on the circumference touches P each time. Keep folding until an ellipse appears.

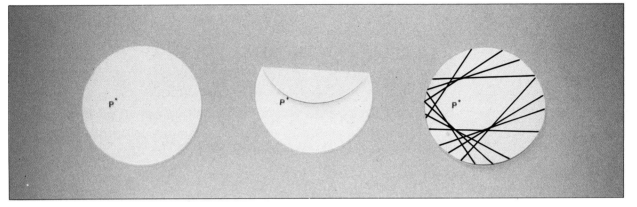

Investigation

● What happens as you move P nearer or further away from the center? What happens when P and the center coincide?

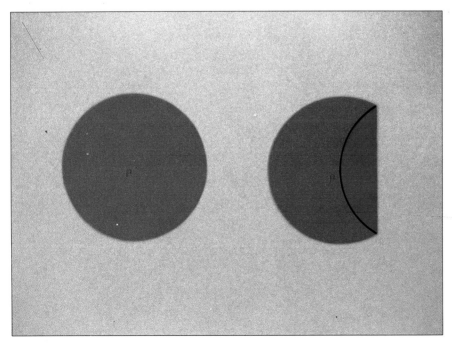

22

A square from circles

The dark shape in the center of this pattern of overlapping circles is called a regular **hexagon**. It has 6 sides of the same length. Figure 1 should help you to figure out how the pattern was made.

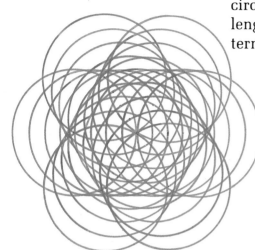

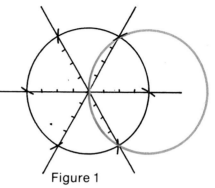

Figure 1

Challenge

Can you make a similar pattern where the shape at the center is a square?

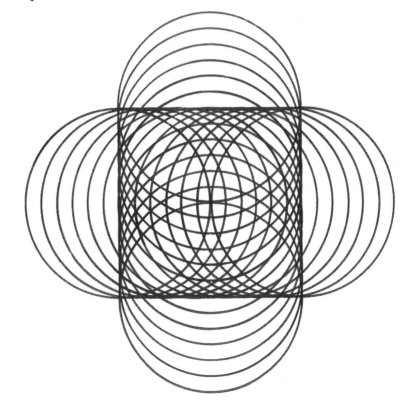

Drawing a cardioid

Cardiology is the study of how the heart works. What does its shape remind you of?

You can form the cardioid from a series of circles.

1. Draw a circle with a radius of 1″. Use a compass to mark off 6 times around the circle. Mark the midpoints to make twelve points on the circumference.

2. Choose one of these points as the point through which all the circles you are about to draw will pass.

3. Draw a series of circles. Use the other 11 points in turn as the center for a circle which passes through your chosen point.

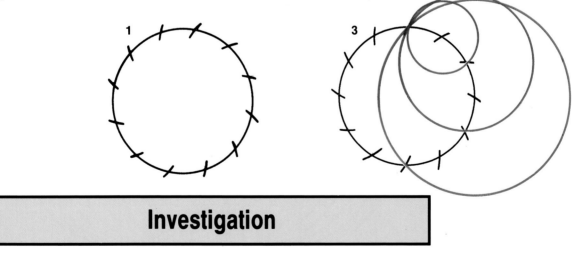

Investigation

● What happens if you increase or decrease the number of points you mark on the circumference?

Challenge

Study the diagram and see if you can produce a nephroid.

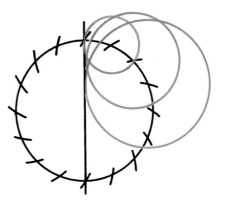

"Nephros" is the Greek word for "kidney" and a nephroid is a kidney-shaped curve in the same way as the cardioid is a heart-shaped curve.

Investigating Cusps

A **cusp** is the point where curved lines meet. The cardioid has one cusp, the nephroid two.

● How many cusps does a trefoil have?

To form the outline of the cardioid (one cusp), you drew circles which all touched a point on the circumference. For the nephroid (two cusps), the circles touched one line.

● How would you form the outline of a trefoil using lines and circles? If you study this drawing, you can figure it out. Produce a trefoil of your own by this method.

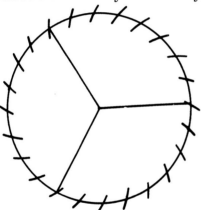

● What would happen if the circles touched one point which was NOT on the circumference? Try to reproduce these outlines.

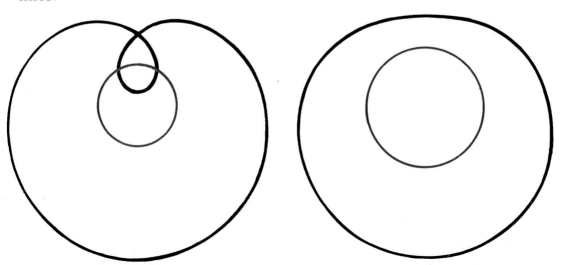

Investigating Envelopes

An alternative to building up shapes by overlapping circles is to form their envelopes with straight lines. You have already used a variation of this method of drawing or folding to form circles and ellipses. (Pages 11 and 22)

To form the envelope of a cardioid

1. Draw a circle with a radius of 2″. Use a protractor to mark off 36 points on the circumference of 10 degrees each. Number them 1 to 36.

2. With a ruler, draw lines joining up the points using the 2 times table.

    point 1 to point 2
    point 2 to point 4
    point 3 to point 6 and so on.

3. When you get to point 19, add on from 36
    $19 \times 2 = 38 = 36 + 2$
    so join point 19 to point 2
    point 20 to point 4 and so on until you reach point 35.
    Point 36 joins onto itself.

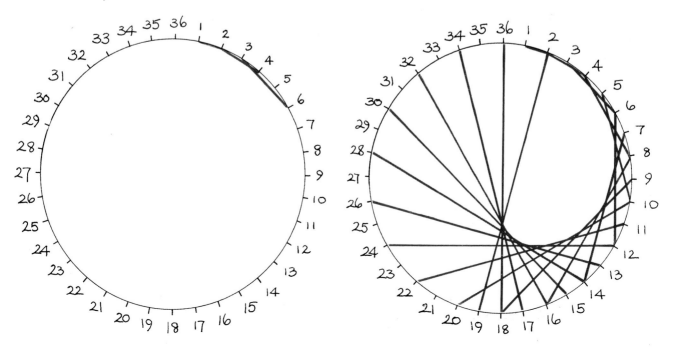

Draw another circle and mark it off as before. Experiment with the 3 times table.

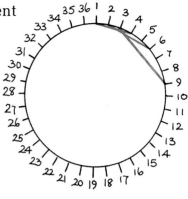

28

You should have produced a shape like this once before.

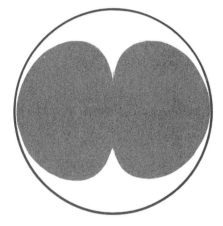

● What is the name of this shape?

> **Look back at page 25 if you have forgotten the name of the shape.**

● How do you think you could use circles, lines and multiplication tables to form these shapes?

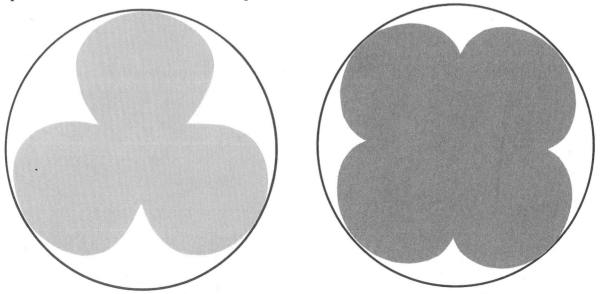

Investigation

● What envelopes are formed if you add to each point instead of multiplying?

The pattern below shows the start of the envelope formed by adding 4.

Point 1 joins to point 5 (add on 4)
Point 2 joins to point 6
and so on.

Twenty four points marked off around the circumference are sufficient for this investigation. You need to measure 15° at a time. (360 ÷ 24 = 15)

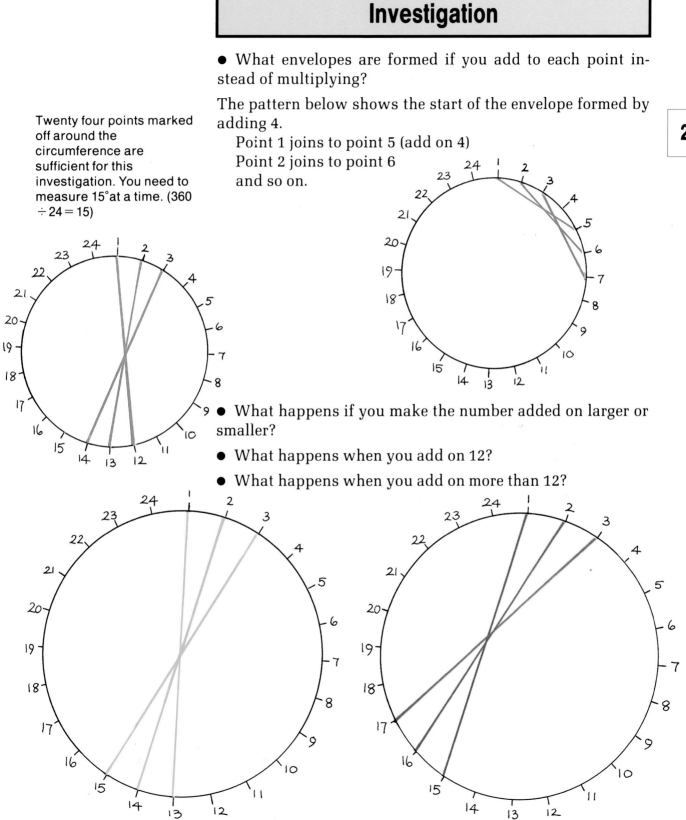

● What happens if you make the number added on larger or smaller?

● What happens when you add on 12?

● What happens when you add on more than 12?

● Can you copy this pattern?

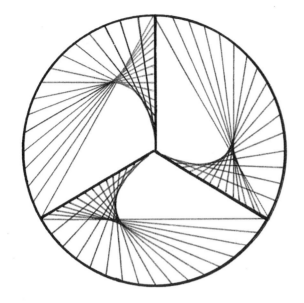

● Try some designs of your own. If you find one you like, you could turn it into a picture or cushion cover by stitching it with thread instead of drawing lines with pencil. Black thread on a white background shows up well, or you can experiment with colors.

These lines and numbers should help you.

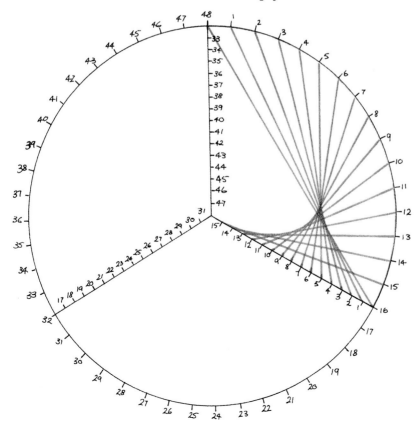

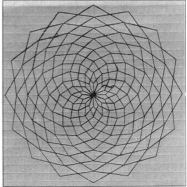

Investigating Jumping Around Circles

You need – plain paper, a protractor, a ruler and pencil.

● Draw a circle with a radius of 3". Mark off the circumference into 8 equal sections (45 degrees each) and number them 1 to 8.

1. Starting at 1, jump 4 spaces to number 5. Join points 1 and 5 with a straight line. Jump 4 spaces from number 5. What number do you reach? What two shapes have you made inside the circle?·

2. In a different color pen, or in a new circle, draw in the results of jumping around the circle 2 spaces at a time?

3. What is the name of the shape produced when you go around the circle jumping 1 space at a time?

4. What happens when you jump 3 spaces each time? (Keep going until you get back to 1.)

● How else can you get the same pattern?

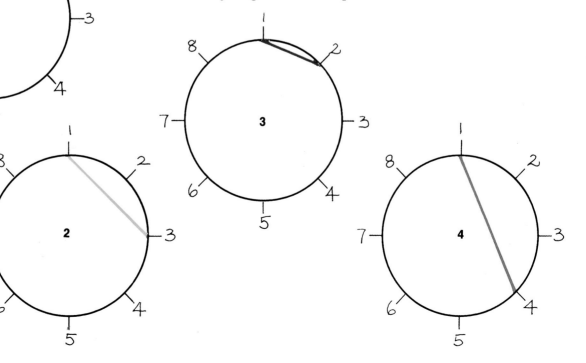

These four diagrams show the results you should have gotten.

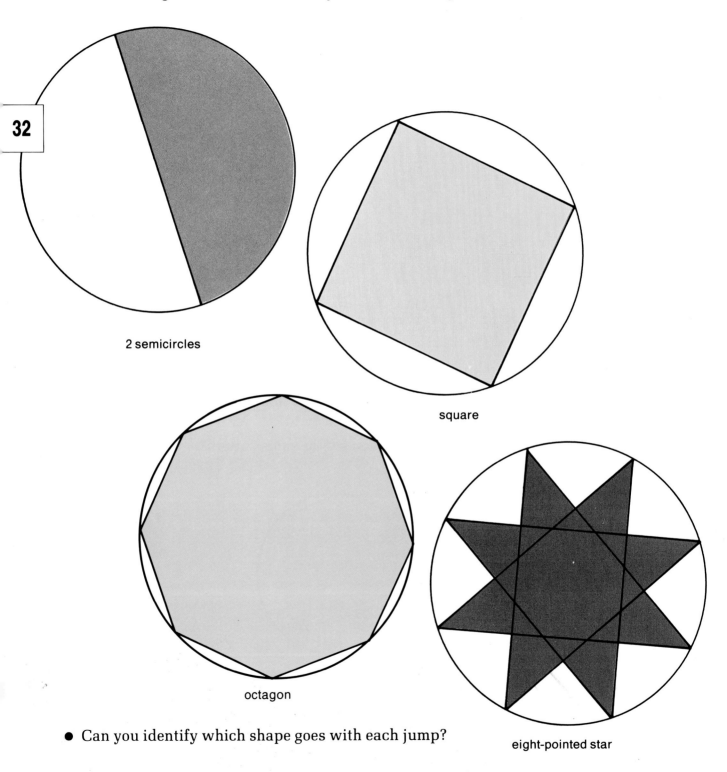

2 semicircles

square

octagon

eight-pointed star

● Can you identify which shape goes with each jump?

● Investigate different jumps with 12 points around a circle.

☆ **Hint:** $\frac{360}{12} = 30$

You will be able to spot patterns and predict results more easily if you work methodically and record your results clearly.

One possibility is to start with jumping 1 space, then 2 spaces, then 3 and so on, recording your results in a table like this:

Number of Jumps	Shape Produced
1	Dodecagon
2	

The names of the shapes produced are shown below.

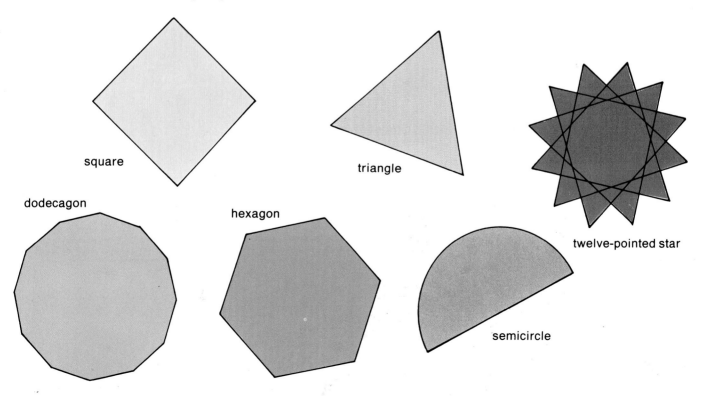

square

triangle

dodecagon

hexagon

semicircle

twelve-pointed star

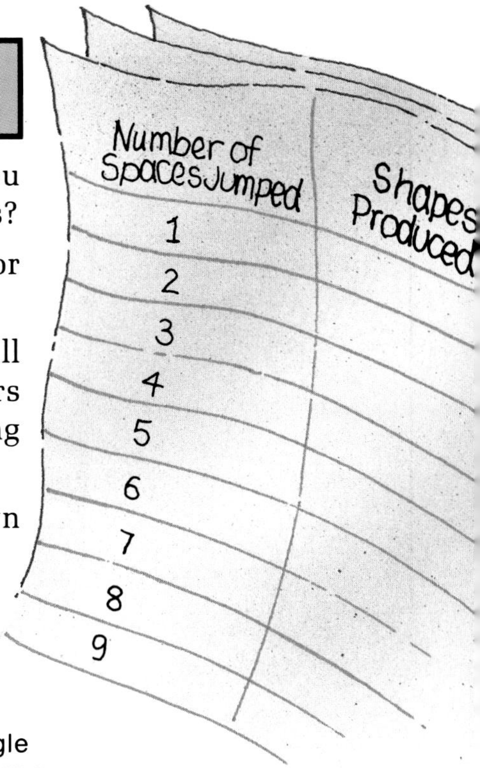

Challenge

• Using your results for circles with 8 and 12 points, can you predict the results of jumping around a circle with 10 points?

Look ahead to pages 35 and 36 to check that your results for circles with 12 points were correct.

Try to fill in your table of results without having to draw all the circles. Some of them you may know right away. Others you will be able to fill in once you spot the pattern building up in the table.

The names of the new shapes you will produce are shown below.

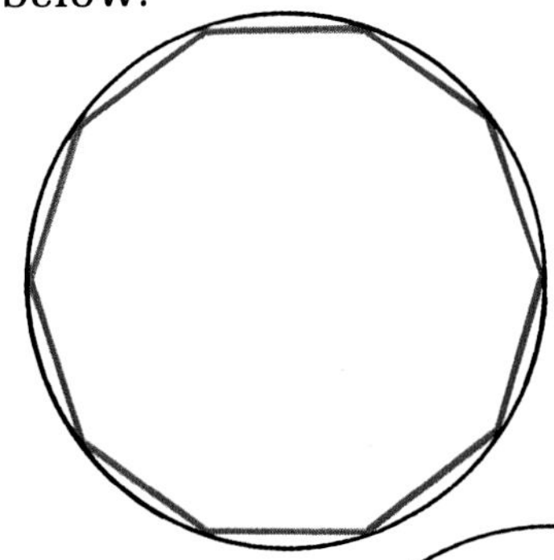

Number of Spaces Jumped	Shapes Produced
1	
2	
3	
4	
5	
6	
7	
8	
9	

decagon

pentangle or pentagram

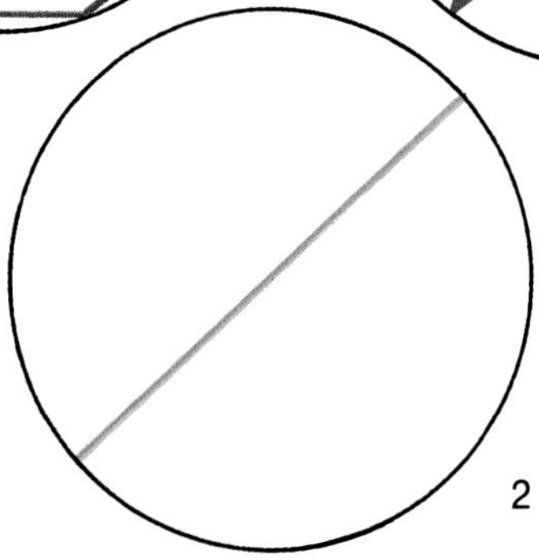

2 semicircles

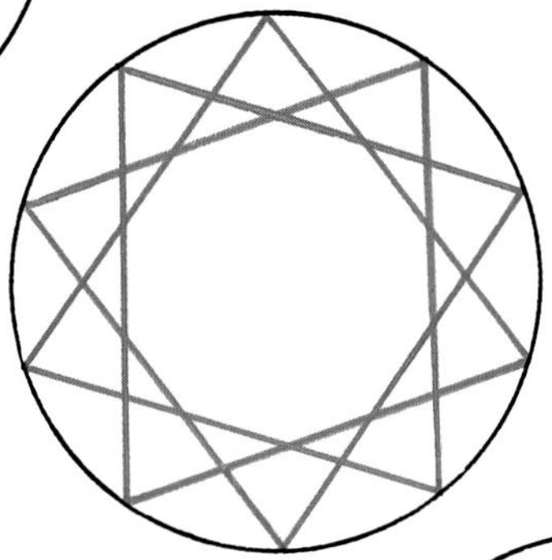

ten-pointed star

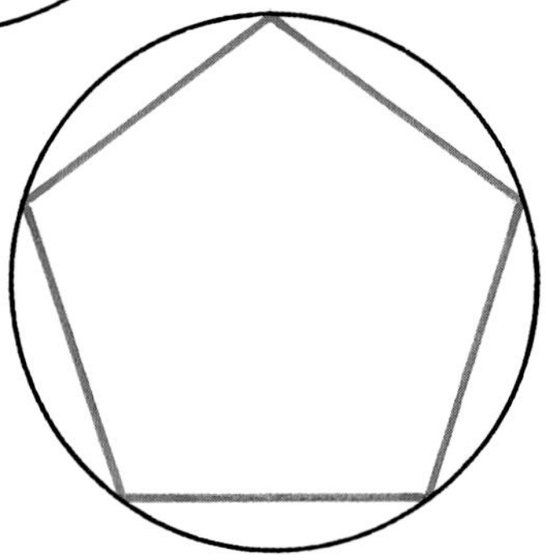

pentagon

• If you are good at computer programming, or have a graphics program which will allow you to produce circles and jumps easily on a computer, you can investigate further. See if you can recognize any rules about producing shapes with circles and jumps.

Turn to page 47.

Results for a circle with 12 points	
Number of spaces jumped	Shape produced
1	Dodecagon
2	Hexagon
3	Square
4	Triangle
5	12 pointed star
6	Semi circle
7	12 pointed star
8	Triangle
9	Square
10	Hexagon
11	Dodecagon

The results for a circle with 12 marked points on the circumference.

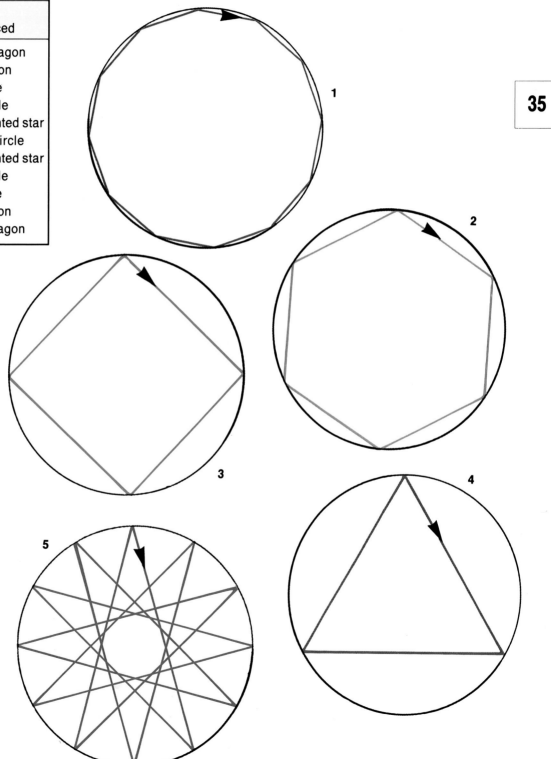

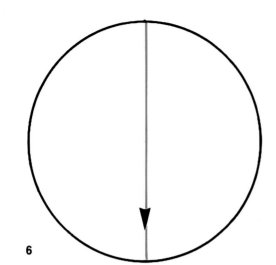

6

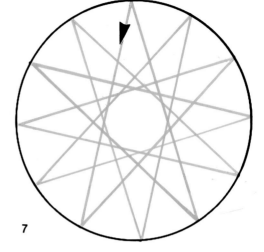

7

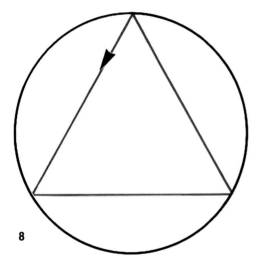

8

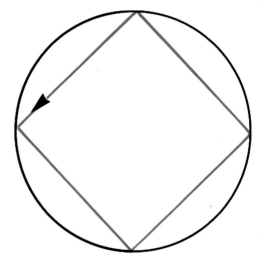

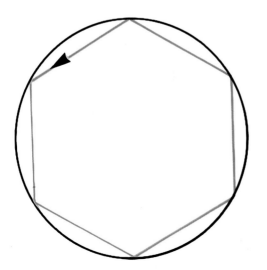

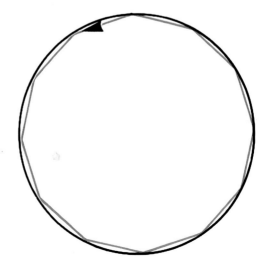

Circles and Symmetry

● Can you see what these shapes have in common?

They all have a line of symmetry. When you can put a mirror down the middle of a shape and one half is an exact reflection of the other, we say that the shape has a line of symmetry. Another way to find a line of symmetry is to fold. If one half fits exactly on to the other, the fold is a line of symmetry.

Some shapes have more than one line of symmetry. How many lines of symmetry do these shapes have? Either test them with a mirror or trace and fold them.

Adding a pattern can make a difference. Look at the symmetry in these patterned shapes.

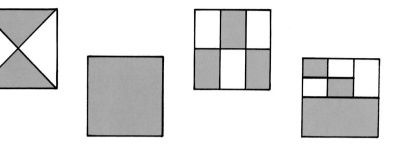

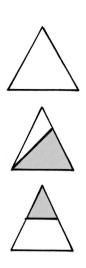

If we look at a plain circle with no pattern, the diameter is a line of symmetry. This means that a circle has an infinite number of lines of symmetry. If you are not sure why, look back at Pages 8 and 9.

When we add a pattern to the circle, the number of lines of symmetry is reduced. How many lines of symmetry do these circle patterns have?

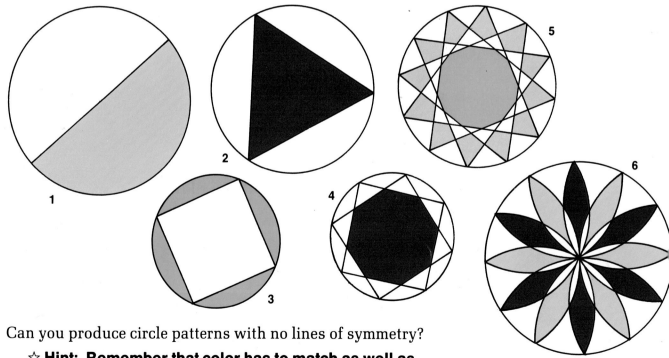

Can you produce circle patterns with no lines of symmetry?

☆ **Hint: Remember that color has to match as well as shape if a pattern has line symmetry.**

38

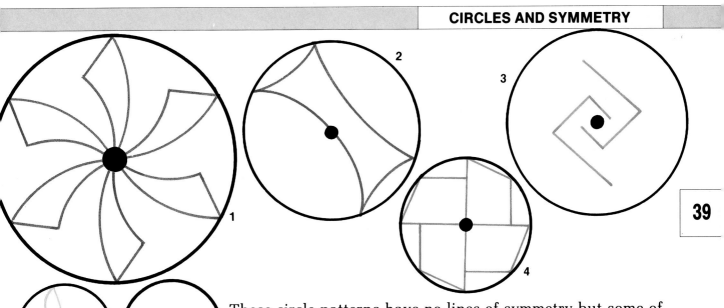

These circle patterns have no lines of symmetry but some of them have rotational symmetry.

● Make a tracing of each pattern. With a pin, fasten the tracing over the drawings so that the patterns match. Slowly rotate the tracing and make a note of how many positions there are when the tracing exactly matches the drawing.

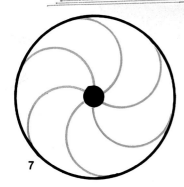

The number of positions where the tracing fits is called the order of rotational symmetry.

● What is the order of rotational symmetry of the shapes and patterns at the top of the page?

The order of rotational symmetry of a plain circle must be infinite. You could move your tracing an infinite number of ways to make it fit the circle underneath.

Measuring Circles

Measuring the circumference

40

1. How would you measure the circumference of this circle?

2. Of a can?

3. Of a bicycle wheel
still attached to the frame?

4. Of a button?

● Which will give you the most accurate result?

1. A piece of string and a ruler?

2. A strip of paper, a pin and a ruler?

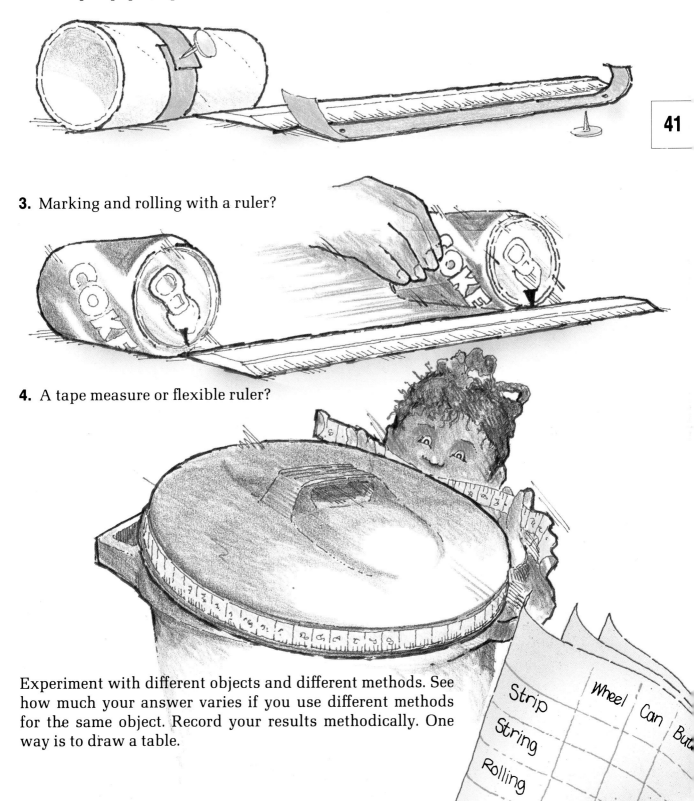

3. Marking and rolling with a ruler?

4. A tape measure or flexible ruler?

Experiment with different objects and different methods. See how much your answer varies if you use different methods for the same object. Record your results methodically. One way is to draw a table.

Strip
String
Rolling

Wheel   Can   But

Measuring the diameter

One way to measure the diameter is to measure from one point on the circumference to another with the ruler passing through the center. If the center is not marked and it is not practical to fold the circle, there are other ways of finding its center.

42

● Perhaps the easiest is to trace the circle, fold it and use it as a pattern to mark the original circle's center with a pin.

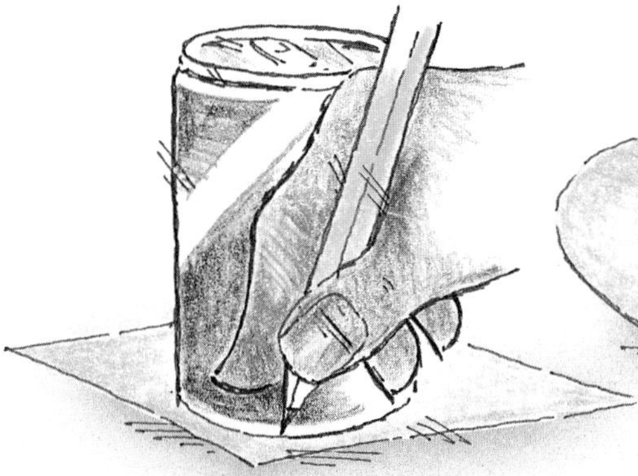

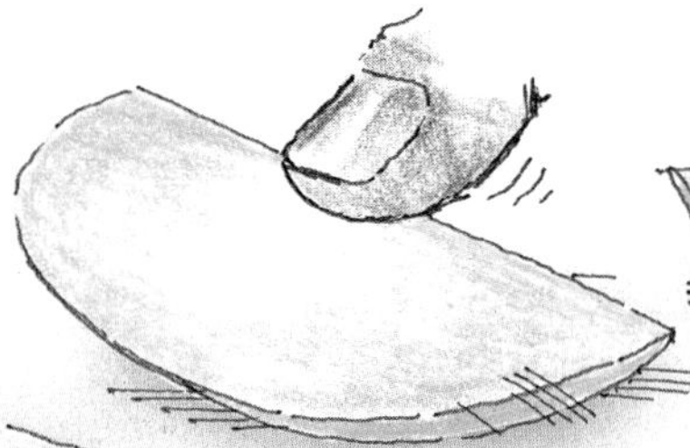

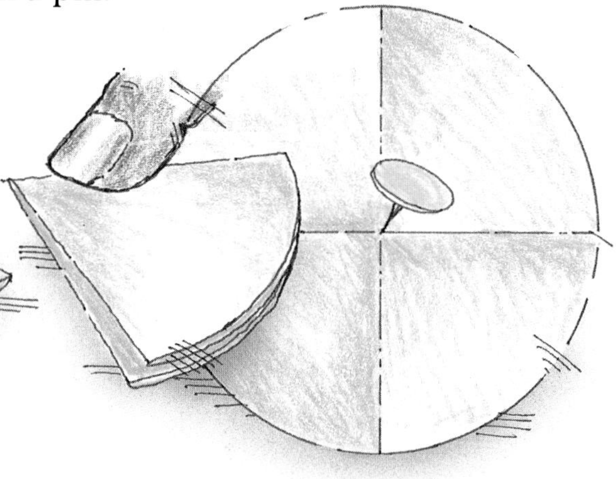

● You can also use a compass to find the center of a drawn circle.

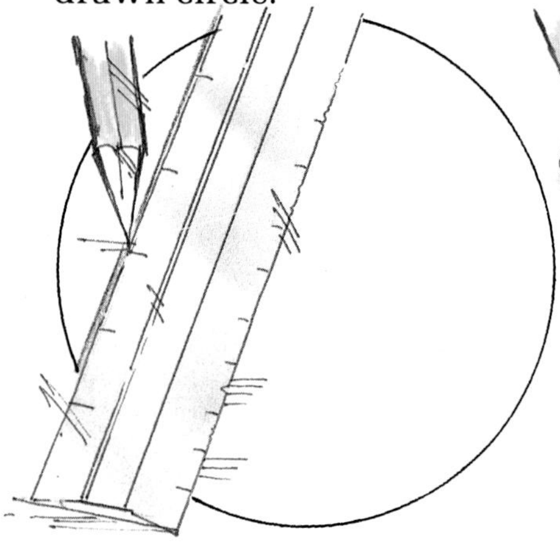

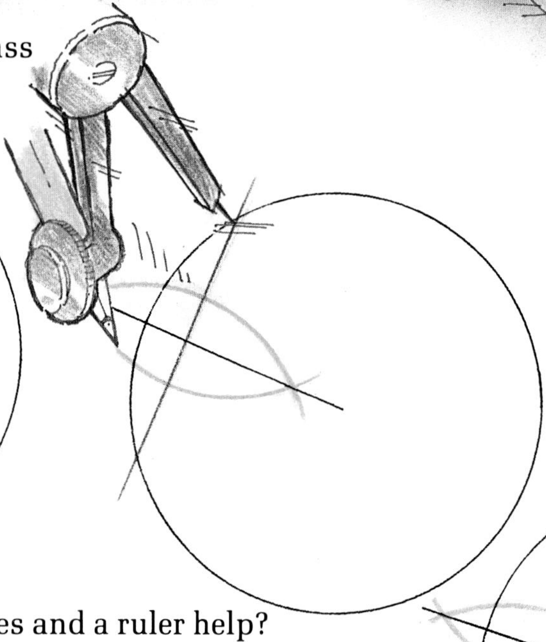

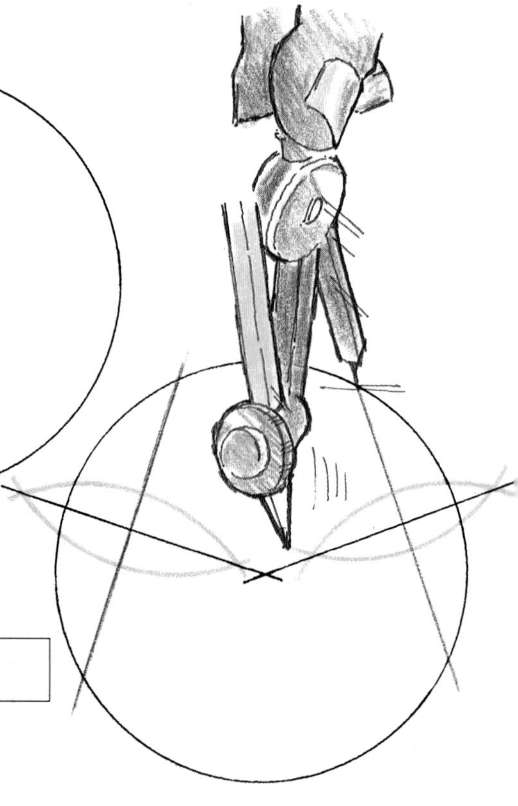

● How could two set squares and a ruler help?

● What are **calipers**?

Turn to page 47.

Circles and the ancient Egyptians

Mathematics was important to the ancient Egyptians. They needed to be able to measure areas accurately because the boundary stones marking the ownership of tracts of land were washed away every year in the annual Nile River flood.

The ancient Egyptians knew how to figure out the area of a shape with straight sides by dividing it into triangles. Shapes with curved edges caused them problems until nearly four thousand years ago. In the nineteenth century B.C., they found out an interesting fact about the lengths of the diameter and circumference of any circle.

44

Investigation

● Find a selection of circles of various sizes such as a coin, a bicycle wheel, the base of a can, various plates, a garbage can lid, a button, the bottom of a pencil and the top of a waste paper basket. You need about ten objects.

Object	Circumference	Diameter
	22"	7"
Wheel	31½	10"
Clock		
Plate		

● Carefully measure the length of the circumference and diameter of each object and record your results in a table as shown. Select a method of measuring which is appropriate to the object. See pages 40 to 42 and your results table.

● Look carefully at your table of results and see if you can find the relationship between the diameter and circumference of any circle which the Egyptian scribes knew.

Testing your theory

● What is the approximate circumference of a circle:
   1. Of diameter 1"?
   2. Of radius 3"?

● If the Equator measures approximately 24,000 miles, about how far is it to the center of the Earth?

Turn to Page 47.

The Greeks and the Magic of Pi

It was discovered about 400 B.C. that there are some numbers which cannot be found by dividing two other numbers. Mathematicians call these irrational numbers. An irrational number is infinite: its decimal places go on forever. You cannot draw a line which is exactly the length of an irrational number. Pi, the relationship between the diameter and the circumference of a circle, is an irrational number. This is why it is represented by a symbol, π; we can never know its absolute value. π has been calculated to more than a billion decimal places by a computer, although we are unlikely ever to need this degree of accuracy.

$\pi = 3 \cdot 141592 \ldots \ldots$

The Babylonians and the Jews were quite happy with the idea that the circumference of a circle is about three times the length of the diameter. You can read evidence of this in the Bible, 1 Kings 7 : 23.

The Egyptians knew that the circumference of a circle was the diameter multiplied by "3 and a bit."

The Greeks wanted to be more precise and to know how big the "bit" was. One of them, Archimedes, worked hard on the problem. Archimedes was a famous mathematician and engineer. His screw, a device for raising water, is still in use in parts of Egypt today. Born in Syracuse in about 287 B.C., he probably went to Egypt as a young man to learn about mathematics and engineering. He was killed in 212 B.C. when the conquering Roman army overran the city of Syracuse.

Archimedes discovered that the value of π lies between $3\frac{1}{7}$ and $3\frac{11}{71}$. For most calculations today, we use his value of $\frac{22}{7}$ or the decimal $3\cdot1416$. We can use a simplified version of his method of finding these values.

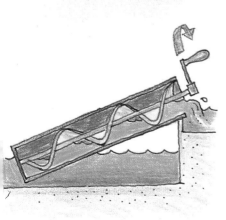

1. Draw accurately a 4″ square. Use a set square. See Page 21 for how to make one if you do not have one.

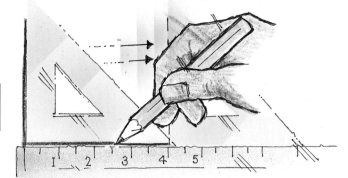
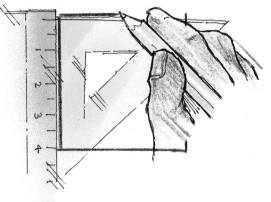

● How long is the perimeter of the square?

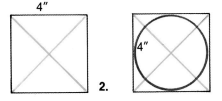

2.

2. Find the square's center by lightly drawing in the diagonals. Use the center to draw with a compass a circle with a diameter of 4″ which just touches the square.

● How many times longer is the square's perimeter than the diameter of the circle?

3. By stepping off with the compass around the circumference (see Page 16), draw a hexagon inside the circle touching the circumference.

● What is the length of the perimeter of the hexagon?

Remember that a hexagon is made from 6 equilateral triangles.

● How many times longer than the diameter of the circle is the perimeter of the hexagon?

The circumference of the circle is shorter than the perimeter of the square and longer than the perimeter of the hexagon. So what do we know about the circumference of the circle compared to its diameter?

Turn to page 48 to check your answers.

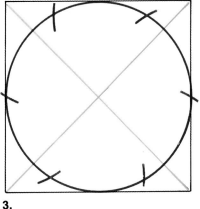

3.

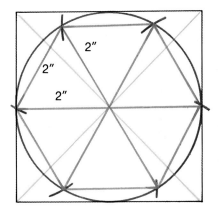

46

Answers to page 34

The results for jumps around a circle with 10 equally spaced points on the circumference.

Number of spaces jumped	Shape produced
1	Decagon
2	Pentagon
3	Ten-pointed star
4	Pentangle
5	Semicircles
6	Pentangle
7	Ten-pointed star
8	Pentagon
9	Decagon

Turn back to page 37.

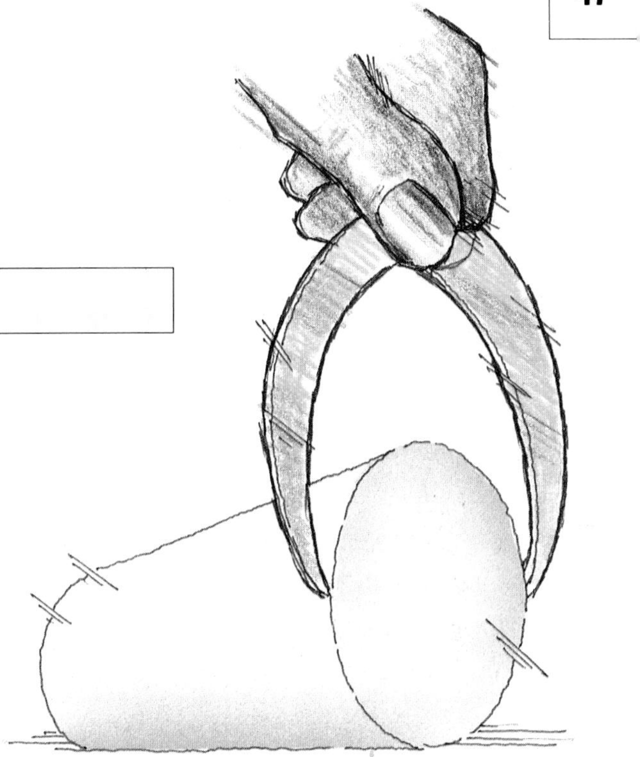

47

Answers to page 42

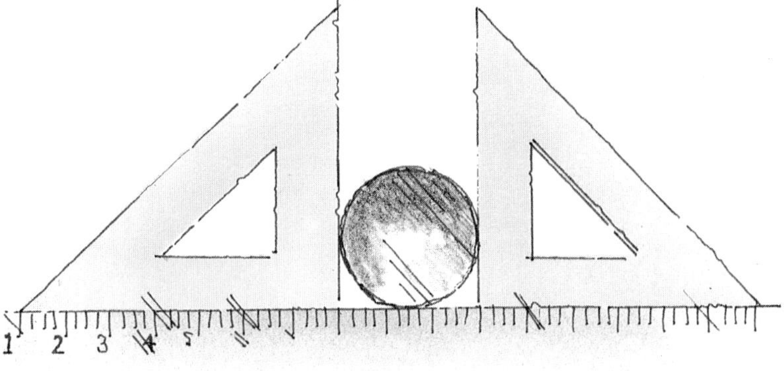

Turn back to page 43.

Answers to page 44

1. 3″ **2.** 18″

About 4,000 miles ($\frac{24000}{6}$)

If you did not get these right, check your circle measurements and try adding this column to your table.

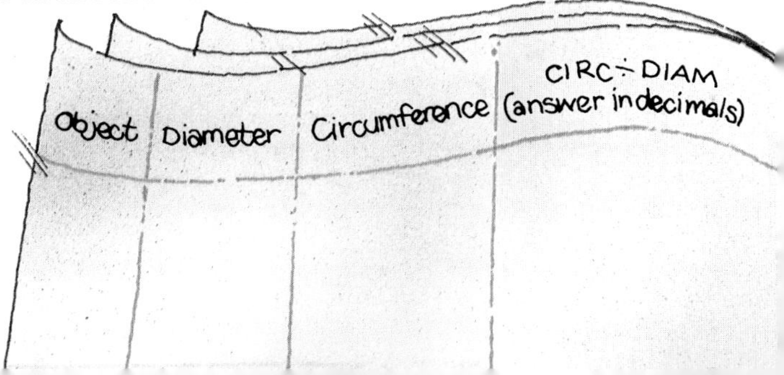

Turn back to page 45.

Object	Diameter	Circumference	CIRC ÷ DIAM (answer in decimals)

Answers to page 46

The perimeter of the square was 16″ (4″ × 4)

The square's perimeter is four times longer than the diameter of the circle.

The perimeter of the hexagon was 12″ (2″ × 6)

The hexagon's perimeter is three times longer than the diameter of the circle.

The diameter of the circle was 4″ (because it touched the sides of the square).

$$16 = 4 \times 4$$
$$12 = 3 \times 4$$

The length of the circumference of the circle was between the lengths of the perimeters of the square and of the hexagon.

Therefore the circumference of a circle must be less than 4 times and more than 3 times as long as its diameter.

If you did not get this right, try again with a square with sides 6″ long. Check your results on Page 63.

Archimedes got more accurate results by drawing polygons with more sides. If you draw an octagon accurately and measure its sides carefully, you should find that the circumference of the circle is less than $3\frac{1}{4}$ times and more than 3 times the diameter.

The circumference of a circle is π times its diameter.

$$C = \pi D \text{ or } C = 2\pi r$$

Archimedes used 96-sided polygons to get his final results!

The Area of a Circle

If you wanted to seed a circular lawn, you would need to know the area of the circle before you bought the seed. For this purpose it would be accurate enough to figure out the area of the square around the circle and say that the area of the circle is "a bit less."

• How would you estimate, by a different method, the area of this circle drawn on graph paper?

By combining these two methods, you can make a more accurate estimate of the area of a circle.

50

Figure	Number of squares in the square	Number of squares in the circle	Fraction
1			
2			
3			
4			
5			
6			

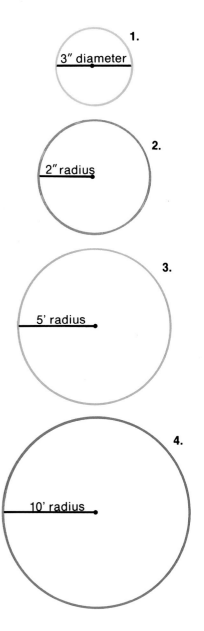

1.
3" diameter

2.
2" radius

3.
5' radius

4.
10' radius

1. For each of the figures above, count the number of small squares in each large square and in each circle. Combine parts of squares to make whole ones. Divide the number of squares in the circle by the number of squares in the square to find the area of the circle as a fraction of the area of the square. Use a calculator if possible.

2. Record your results in a table like the one shown above.

● About what fraction of the area of the square is the area of the circle? The last column in your table tells you.

Use the fact that the area of a circle is about $\frac{3}{4}$ of the area of a square, when the sides are the same length as the circle's diameter, to calculate the approximate areas of the circles shown right. If you use a calculator, $\frac{3}{4} = 0.75$.

● Check your answers at the back of the book.

Polygons and the area of a circle

You could also use the method of drawing many-sided polygons to get two areas between which the area of the circle must lie. This is the same method Archimedes used to get very close to the value of π so that he could calculate the circumference of a circle if he knew the radius. The disadvantage of this is that either you must draw and measure extremely accurately or do some difficult calculations.

Investigating sectors and area

An easier method of calculating the area of a circle is to think about dividing a circle into sectors and rearranging them.

1. On a piece of paper which you can cut up, draw a circle with a radius of 2″. Cut it out and fold it to divide it into 8 equal sectors.

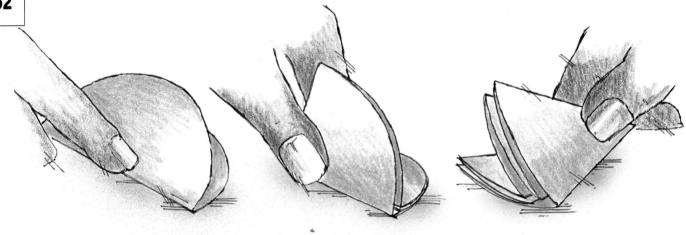

2. Carefully cut out the 8 sectors and rearrange them side by side as shown. Take the first sector, cut it in half and place half at each end. You have now made a shape like a rectangle but with wavy edges at the top and bottom.

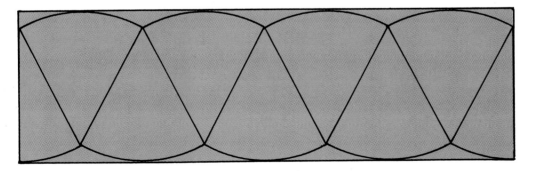

The height of the "rectangle" is approximately the radius of the circle. (The sloping edges of each sector are the radius.)

What about the length of the "rectangle?" All the curved edges of the sectors made the circumference of the circle. Half of them are at the top of the "rectangle" and half at the bottom.

We could say that the "rectangle" has a height r and a length $\frac{1}{2}$ C, where r = the radius of the circle and C = the circumference of the circle.

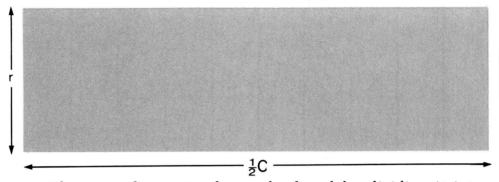

$\frac{1}{2}$C

The area of a rectangle can be found by dividing it into squares and counting them, as can the area of any shape. But because of its shape it is easier and quicker to multiply the height by the length.

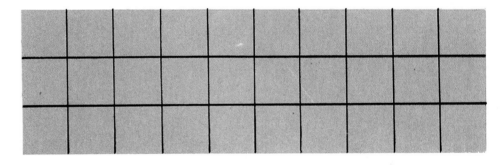

The area of our sector "rectangle" is
   $r \times \frac{1}{2}$ C
but we know that C = 2 π r (page 48)
   therefore $\frac{1}{2}$ C = π r
so the area also = r × π r
this is usually written as
   A = π r^2

Since our sector "rectangle" is only the original circle cut out and rearranged πr^2 must be the area of the circle as well. This gives us a formula that we can use for any circle. As long as we know the radius, we can calculate the area.

The area of a circle = πr^2

The more sectors we cut the more like a true rectangle the rearranged shape becomes. Try just cutting and folding 4 segments. If you have a protractor, you can try making 18 sectors. ($\frac{360}{18} = 20$)

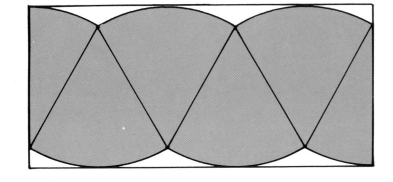

Try to calculate these areas. It is best to use a calculator. If the calculator has a π button, use it. Otherwise use $\pi = 3.14$

● What is the area of a circle with a
1. radius of 3"
2. radius of 4.5"
3. diameter of 1 foot
4. radius of 5 feet 2"
5. diameter of 6.3"

● These shapes are all formed from circles with a diameter of 1" or 2". Calculate their areas as fractions of π.

Above: The more sectors you make, the flatter the rectangle becomes.

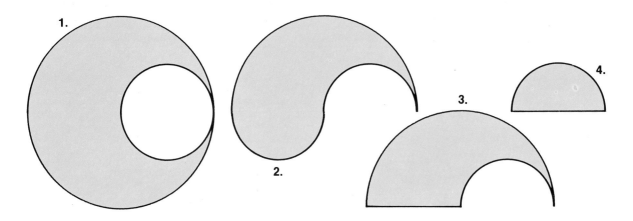

Circles, Areas and Other Shapes

Squaring the circle

A problem which the early Greek mathematicians tried to solve was to draw a square which had exactly the same area as a given circle. For example, if you draw a circle with a radius of 3″ what would be the length of the side of a square to give exactly the same area.

Although they persevered for many centuries students and scholars never succeeded in drawing the elusive square which they sought. Modern mathematicians have proved that it is impossible because π is an irrational number.

Circles and triangles

Archimedes showed that the area of a circle is equal to the area of a triangle. The base of the triangle is equal to the circumference of the circle and the height of the triangle is equal to the radius of the circle.

The area of a triangle $= \frac{1}{2}$ base × height

$\frac{1}{2} C \times r$

but $C = 2\pi r$

therefore area of triangle $= \frac{1}{2} \times 2 \pi r \times r$

$= \pi r^2$

but the area of the circle $= \pi r^2$

therefore the area of the triangle = the area of the circle.

Investigation

1. You need: a piece of string knotted to produce a loop 12″ long and a piece of $\frac{1}{2}$″ graph paper.

2. Drop the string on the paper, flatten it out and count the number of squares which are enclosed by the string. There will be several pieces of squares; pair these up to make nearly whole squares and count them as well.

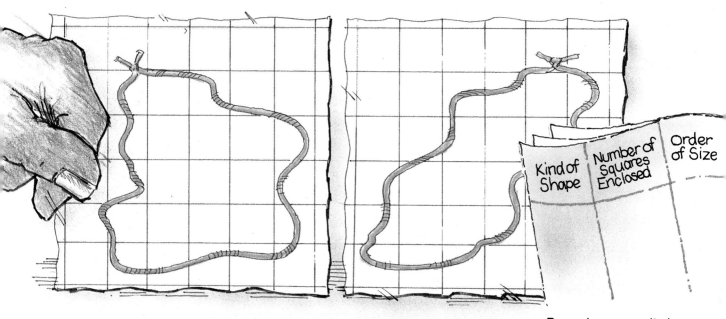

Kind of Shape	Number of Squares Enclosed	Order of Size

Record your results in a table like this.

3. When you have tried several random, irregular shapes, experiment with differently shaped rectangles, polygons and ellipses. Try a square and a circle as well.

4. Look carefully at your results.

● A treasure island is to be sold off in lots which can be enclosed with 1,000 yards of fencing. What would be the best shape to arrange your fencing in to give you the most land and therefore the greatest chance of finding the treasure?

56

The Importance of Circles

Man-made circles

At the beginning of this book you were asked to make lists of circular objects. One which is very common, and which has had far reaching effects on man's civilization, is the wheel.

The wheel was discovered about six thousand years ago in ancient Mesopotamia, a land between the Tigris and Euphrates rivers in what is today called the Middle East. The first wheels were solid discs of wood with a hole in the middle for an axle.

The wheel is not only important as an efficient means of transport; it can be used to harness and control energy. The Mesopotamians also used the potter's wheel and pulley wheels. Potters use wheels to help them to make smooth, strong, symmetrical shapes from one piece of clay. Before the invention of the potter's wheel, the clay had to be rolled into long sausages. These were coiled around on top of each other and smoothed over. Even with this method, objects such as cups and containers tended to be rounded and have circular rims. You can try drinking from a carton of milk with a square top, but it won't be easy.

Pulley wheels can help to lift heavy objects when used to make a block and tackle. They can also transfer power as the fan belt of an automobile does. Mill wheels use the energy in moving water to power machinery.

The circle is a shape frequently used in engineering and manufacturing. It is a strong shape as there are no weak points like the edges of a cube. Circles and cylinders are easy to produce with the help of a lathe, which is the oldest machine tool. One was painted on an Egyptian tomb in 300 B.C.

58

Gears are wheels with teeth cut into them. They are used to transmit power. The gears in a car transmit the power from the engine to the axles to turn the wheels. By varying the number of teeth, you can increase or decrease the speed at which the gear turns.

Spirograph uses gears to produce patterns.

Circles in nature

If you look at the cross-section of a tree trunk, you can see how its circular shape has grown. It started from a small shoot. Each year it increased its cells all around it. Each ring in the trunk represents a year's growth.

However hard we look. we will not find any true circles in nature or in factories. Circles have no thickness; they are two-dimensional; they have a radius and a circumference. A circle with thickness or height is a cylinder.

Also neither nature nor man can produce a circle where every point on the circumference is exactly the same distance from the center. Think about the cross-section of a tree trunk. The bark will be rough. The skin of an orange is pitted. If you cut across an apple the skin will be much smoother but look under a microscope and measure accurately and it will not be a true circle. People can now make circular objects so that to the human eye they appear to be true circles but there will always be minute distortions.

From your work with this book you should now have some understanding of what mathematicians mean by circles. We can explain the idea of a circle in two ways.

● Think back to the ways that you drew circles. The thumbtack, cardboard and pencil method; the two sticks and string and the compass. All of these use the idea that a circle is the path made by an object moving at a fixed distance from another object.

60

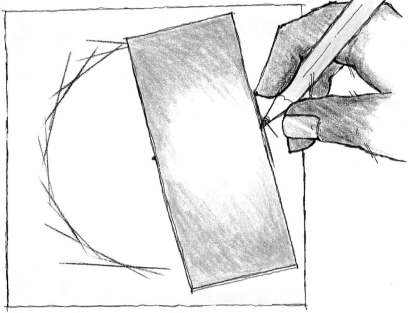

● Another way of producing a circle is to draw or fold a series of straight lines at a fixed distance from a given point. These lines are called the tangents to the circle. A circle has an infinite number of tangents just as it has an infinite number of radii and diameters.

The more you think about them the more fascinating circles are.

Glossary

calipers instruments with curved legs for measuring curved distances

circumference the distance around the edge of a circle

concentric having the same center

cusp the point where two curves meet

decagon a ten-sided polygon

diameter the distance from one point on the circumference of a circle to another, passing through the center

dodecagon a twelve-sided polygon

envelope a shape formed inside a series of lines or curves

hexagon a six-sided polygon

octagon an eight-sided polygon

parallel always the same distance apart

pentangle or pentagram a regular five-pointed star

perimeter the distance around the edge of a shape

perpendicular a line drawn at right angles to another

polygon a closed shape made of straight lines

radius the distance from the center of a circle to the edge

regular polygon a polygon with all its sides the same length and all its angles the same size

sphere a solid shaped like a ball

three-dimensional having length, width and depth

Answers

Page 8 1. Diameter $= 4''$ **2.** Radius $= 6''$

Page 9 Yes, a diameter is a special chord, one which passes through the center of the circle.
   The least number of folds you need is 2. The fold line is the diameter.
   It works wherever you place the marks.

Page 11 Use a thinner or thicker ruler. The width of the ruler is the radius of the circle. In the folding method the strip of paper takes the place of the ruler. The folds build up the circumference of the circle in the same way as the pencil lines.

Page 22 The nearer the point P is to the center the more circular the ellipse is. When the point P is at the center the shape produced is a circle.

Page 23 Forming a square from circles. Draw a pair of perpendiculars. Draw a series of circles of equal radius along each arm.

Page 24 The cardioid is heart-shaped. Increasing the number of points makes the outline smoother.

Page 26

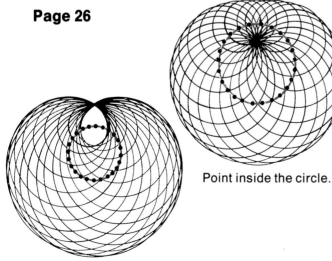

Point inside the circle.

Point outside the circle.

Page 28 The shape is a nephroid. The 3 times table produces the envelope of a nephroid. The 4 times table produces a three-cusped shape. The 5 times table produces a four-cusped shape.

Page 29 The envelope of a circle is produced. When adding on numbers from 1 to 11 its radius decreases as the number added on increases. When 12 is added on the radius is zero. When a number larger than 12 is added the radius increases as the number added on increases.

Pages 31 and 32 The results for an 8 point circle are:

Jump 1 octagon.   Jump 3 eight-pointed star.
Jump 2 square.   Jump 4 semicircles.

You can also get an eight-pointed star by jumping five.

Page 34 See page 47

Page 37 The shield has 1 line of symmetry
The shamrock leaf has 2 lines of symmetry.
The snowflake has 6 lines of symmetry.

Page 38

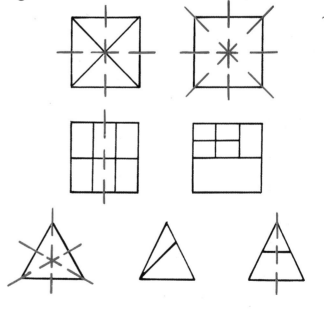

1. 1 line of symmetry.
2. 3 lines of symmetry.
3. 4 lines of symmetry.
4. 8 lines of symmetry.
5. 12 lines of symmetry.
6. 6 lines of symmetry.

Page 39 The rotational symmetry of the circles are: No.1. 6, No.2. 1, No.3. 2, No.4. 4, No.5. 3, No.6. 2, No.7. 6.

Page 42 See page 47

Page 44 See page 47

Page 46 See page 48

Page 48 For a square with 6″ sides
the perimeter of the square $= 24″$
the perimeter of the hexagon $= 18″$
$(3″ \times 6″)$
the diameter of the circle $= 6″$
$24 = 4 \times 6$ $\qquad$ $18 = 3 \times 6$
The circumference of the circle is less than 4 times and more than 3 times the length of its diameter.

Page 49 Find the area by counting the squares. Each square $= \frac{1}{4}$ square inch so divide the number of squares by 16 for total number of square inches.

Page 50 1. $\frac{3}{4}$ of 9 sq. in. $= 4\frac{1}{2} + 2\frac{1}{4} = 6\frac{3}{4}$ sq. in.
or 0.75 $\times$ 9 sq. in. $= 6.75$ sq. in.
2. $\frac{3}{4}$ of 16 sq. in. $= 8 + 4 = 12$ sq. in.
or 0.75 $\times$ 16 sq. in. $= 12$ sq. in.
3. $\frac{3}{4}$ of 100 sq. ft. $= 75$ sq. ft.
or 0.75 $\times$ 100 sq. ft. $= 75$ sq. ft.
4. $\frac{3}{4}$ of 400 sq. ft. $= 300$ sq. ft
or 0.75 $\times$ 100 sq. ft. $= 300$ sq. ft.

Page 54 1. $\pi r^2 = 9\pi = 28.7$ sq. in.
$(9 \times 3.14 = 28.26)$
2. $\pi r^2 = 20.25\pi = 63.62$ sq. in.
$(20.25 \times 3.14 = 63.59)$

3. $\pi r^2 = \frac{1}{4}\pi = 0.79$ sq. ft. $(0.25 \times 3.14 = 0.79)$
4. $\pi r^2 = 26.69$ or $5.167^2 = 83.87$ sq. ft. (26.69 or $5.167^2 \times 3.14 = 83.82$ sq. ft.)
5. $\pi r^2 = 26.69$ or $5.167^2 = 31.17$ sq. in. $(9.9225 \times 3.14 = 31.16)$

Answers to diagrams
$R = 1″$ $\quad r = \frac{1}{2}″$
1. $\pi r^2 - \pi(\frac{1}{2}r)^2 = \pi - \frac{1}{4}\pi = \frac{3}{4}\pi$
2. $\frac{1}{2}\pi r^2 = \frac{1}{2} \times \pi \times 1 = \frac{1}{2}\pi$
3. $\frac{1}{2}$ of $\pi r^2 - \frac{1}{2}$ of $\pi(\frac{1}{2}r)^2 = \frac{1}{2} - \frac{1}{8}\pi = \frac{3}{8}\pi$
4. $\frac{1}{2}$ of $\pi r^2 = \frac{1}{2} \times \pi \times \frac{1}{4} = \frac{1}{8}\pi$

Page 56 A circle would give you the best chance because a circle encloses the maximum area for a given perimeter.

63

Index